Live the Mystery

Scriptural Rosary

Selected Scriptural verses
reviewed and approved by,
Reverend Evan A. Howard, O.F.M.

Nihil Obstat: Rev. Thomas Herbst, O.F.M.

Imprimatur: Very Rev. A. Melvin Jurisich, O.F.M.
Provincial
March 12, 2003

The nihil obstat and imprimatur are a declaration that a book or pamphlet is considered to be free from doctrinal and moral error.

Scripture text taken from the Holy Bible, New International Version ®, Copyright © 1973, 1978, 1984
by international Bible Society.

Used by permission of Zondervan Publishing House.
All rights reserved.

The "NIV" and "New International Version" trademarks are registered in the United States Patent and Trademark Office by International Bible Society.

Copyright © 2001, 2002 Rev. Evan A. Howard, O.F.M.

All Rights Reserved

No part of this book may be reproduced or copied in any form or by any means—-graphic, electronic, or mechanical, including photocopying, recording, taping or information storage and retrieval system—-without written permission of the publisher.

Published by: Tau-publishing
Printed in U.S.A.

For reorders and other publications visit us at:
www.tau-publishing.org

ISBN Number 0-9719921-4-2
First Edition April 2003

Introduction

Just as the Life, Death, and Resurrection of Jesus is for the most part a mystery, so too is our own life journey. When we meditate upon the Mysteries of the Rosary and reflect deeply upon them and our own life in relationship to the life of Jesus, we are living the mystery with Him.

If there is anyone who lived that mystery ever so intimately with Jesus it is His mother Mary. When we live the mystery of the life of Jesus and reflect upon our own, we also live it with our Blessed Mother. We stand by her in the joyful mysteries as she is approached by the angel Gabriel. During the visitation and throughout the birth of our Savior we are inspired by her courage and unending faith. We too ponder the words spoken by Simeon as he prophesied about the life of Jesus at the Presentation and are equally perplexed as to how such a young boy could command the attention of the doctors and scholars in the temple.

We stand back with Mary as Jesus is baptized in the Jordan by his cousin John. For the most part, as it is written in Scripture, Mary is quietly off to the side while the life of Jesus unfolds. However, there is one moment at the wedding feast of Cana when Mary comes to the forefront as she very confidently tells Jesus the hosts have run out of wine. Then once more she is a silent observer as our Lord begins His public ministry.

As Mary stands by the cross of her Son, we are there with her. Our hearts ache over what has already happened to Him, only to see it ultimately worsen as Jesus is nailed to the cross where He suffers for an agonizing three hours before He releases His Spirit to His Father.

Before Jesus breathed His last, He looked down from the cross and said to Mary, "Dear woman, here is your son." Then to the disciple, "Here is your mother." Just as John took Mary into his home, so too do we take her into our own hearts as a loving mother, protected always under her mantle.

There is much rejoicing as we see the scriptures take one more step towards fulfillment in Jesus' ascension and the subsequent arrival of the Holy Spirit. After her time on earth is finished, Mary is assumed into heaven where she is crowned the Queen of heaven and earth.

Clearly the Rosary is not a devotion to Mary. It is however one we most definitely pray with her. With each Our Father and Hail Mary we express our deep love for Jesus, and we do it with the utmost respect for the one who gave her fiat to our Father in heaven.

As we walk along our journey, we rejoice in knowing our Blessed Mother is walking with us, leading us at every moment with that same deep maternal love she has for her son, Jesus. It is our mother in heaven who is constantly pointing us in Jesus' direction, just as she said to the servants at Cana, "Do as He tells you."

On the cover we see the cross of Jesus in the center of the Rosary. This is the most important part of living the mystery with our Lord—to place Him in the center of each step we take along the journey. He is the center of the scriptural Rosary and should be the center of our everyday life.

As we open ourselves to the mystery of His Life, Death, and Resurrection by meditating upon the scriptural passages of the Most Holy Rosary, we also open ourselves to the abundant Grace that constantly surrounds us. It is this Grace that allows us to journey not in darkness, but into the true light of our Lord and Savior Jesus Christ.

His mother said to the servants, "Do whatever He tells you."   *John 2:5*

Scriptural Rosary

One mystery of the Scriptural Rosary is recited
as follows:

The joyful Mysteries on Monday and Saturday,

The Mysteries of Light on Thursdays,

The Sorrowful Mysteries on Tuesday and Friday,

The Glorious Mysteries on Wednesday and Sunday,

or, per the order of the seasons.

The Apostles' Creed

I believe in God, the Father Almighty,
creator of heaven and earth,
I believe in Jesus Christ, His only Son, our Lord.
He was conceived by the power of the Holy Spirit,
and born of the Virgin Mary.
He suffered under Pontius Pilate,
was crucified, died, and was buried.
He descended to the dead.
On the third day He rose again.
He ascended into heaven,
and is seated at the right hand of the Father.
He will come again to judge the living and the dead.
I believe in the Holy Spirit,
the Holy Catholic Church,
the communion of saints,
the forgiveness of sins,
the resurrection of the body,
and the life everlasting. Amen.

Our Father

Our Father, who art in heaven
hallowed be thy name;
thy kingdom come;
thy will be done on earth
as it is in heaven.
Give us this day our daily bread
and forgive us our trespasses
as we forgive those
who trespass against us;
and lead us not into temptation,
but deliver us from evil. Amen.

Hail Mary

Hail Mary, full of grace.
The Lord is with you.
Blessed are you among women,
and blessed is the fruit
of your womb, Jesus.
Holy Mary, mother of God,
pray for us sinners,
now and at the hour of our death. Amen.

(three times)

Glory Be

Glory be to the Father, and to the Son, and to the
Holy Spirit.
As it was in the beginning, is now, and ever shall be,
world without end. Amen.

The Joyful Mysteries

First Joyful Mystery

The Annunciation

Our Father

God sent the angel Gabriel to a virgin.
The virgin's name was Mary.

Luke 1:26,27

Hail Mary

"Greetings, you who are highly favored!
The Lord is with you."

Luke 1:28

Hail Mary

Mary was greatly troubled at his words
and wondered what kind of greeting this might be.

Luke 1:29

Hail Mary

"Do not be afraid, Mary,
you have found favor with God."

Luke 1:30

Hail Mary

"You will be with child and give birth to a son,
and you are to give him the name Jesus."

Luke 1:31

Hail Mary

"He will be great and will be called Son of the Most High. He will reign over the house of Jacob forever."

Luke 1:32,33

Hail Mary

"How will this be," Mary asked the angel, "Since I am a virgin?"

Luke 1:34

Hail Mary

"The Holy Spirit will come upon you, and the power of the Most High will over shadow you."

Luke 1:35

Hail Mary

"So the Holy One to be born will be called the Son of God."

Luke 1:35

Hail Mary

"I am the Lord's servant," Mary answered. "May it be to me as you have said."

Luke 1:38

Hail Mary

Glory Be

Glory be to the Father, and to the Son, and to the Holy Spirit.
As it was in the beginning, is now, and ever shall be, world without end. Amen.

Second Joyful Mystery

The Visitation

Our Father

Mary hurried to a town in the hill country of Judea, where she entered Zechariah's home and greeted Elizabeth.

Luke 1:39,40

Hail Mary

When Elizabeth heard Mary's greeting, the baby leaped in her womb, and Elizabeth was filled with the Holy Spirit.

Luke 1:41

Hail Mary

In a loud voice she exclaimed: "Blessed are you among women, and blessed is the child you will bear!"

Luke 1:42

Hail Mary

"Blessed is she who has believed that what the Lord has said to her will be accomplished!"

Luke 1:45

Hail Mary

And Mary said: "My soul glorifies the Lord and my spirit rejoices in God my Saviour."

Luke 1:46,47

Hail Mary

"From now on all generations will call me blessed,
for the Mighty One has done great things for me—
Holy is His name."

Luke 1:48-49

Hail Mary

"His Mercy extends to those who fear Him,
from generation to generation."

Luke 1:50

Hail Mary

"He has performed mighty deeds with His arm; He has scattered those who are proud in their inmost thoughts."

Luke 1:51

Hail Mary

"He has brought down rulers from their thrones
but has lifted up the humble."

Luke 1:52

Hail Mary

"He has filled the hungry with good things
but has sent the rich away empty."

Luke 1:53

Hail Mary

Glory Be

Glory be to the Father, and to the Son, and to the Holy Spirit.
As it was in the beginning, is now, and ever shall be, world without end. Amen.

Third Joyful Mystery

The Nativity

Our Father

Joseph went up from the town of Nazareth to Bethlehem.
He went there with Mary, who was expecting a child.

Luke 2:4,5

Hail Mary

While they were there, the time came
for the Baby to be born.

Luke 2:6

Hail Mary

She gave birth to her firstborn, a son. She wrapped Him
in cloths and placed Him in a manger.

Luke 2:7

Hail Mary

There were shepherds living out in the fields nearby.
An angel of the Lord appeared to them.

Luke 2:8,9

Hail Mary

"Do not be afraid. I bring you good news of great joy that
will be for all the people."

Luke 2:10

Hail Mary

"Today in the town of David a Saviour has been born to you; He is Christ the Lord."

Luke 2:11

Hail Mary

"Glory to God in the highest, and on earth peace to men on whom His favor rests."

Luke 2:14

Hail Mary

After Jesus was born in Bethlehem,
Magi from the east came from Jerusalem.

Matthew 2:1

Hail Mary

They saw the child with his Mother Mary, and they bowed down and worshiped Him.

Matthew 2:11

Hail Mary

Mary treasured up all these things
and pondered them in her heart.

Luke 2:19

Hail Mary

Glory Be

Glory be to the Father, and to the Son, and to the Holy Spirit.
As it was in the beginning, is now, and ever shall be, world without end. Amen.

Fourth Joyful Mystery

The Presentation

Our Father

According to the law of Moses, Joseph and Mary took Him to Jerusalem to present Him to the Lord.

Luke 2:22

Hail Mary

Now there was a man in Jerusalem called Simeon who was righteous and devout.

Luke 2:25

Hail Mary

It had been revealed to him by the Holy Spirit that he would not die before he had seen the Lord's Christ.

Luke 2:26

Hail Mary

When the parents brought in the child, Simeon took Him in his arms and praised God.

Luke 2:27,28

Hail Mary

"Sovereign Lord, as You have promised, You now dismiss your servant in peace."

Luke 2:29

Hail Mary

"For my eyes have seen Your Salvation, which You have prepared in the sight of all people."

Luke 2:30,31

Hail Mary

"A light for revelation to the Gentiles
and for glory to Your people Israel."

Luke 2:32

Hail Mary

Simeon said, "This child is destined to cause the falling and rising of many in Israel, a sign that will be spoken against."

Luke 2:34

Hail Mary

"The thoughts of many hearts will be revealed.
A sword will pierce your own soul too."

Luke 2:35

Hail Mary

They returned to Nazareth. The Child grew and became strong; He was filled with wisdom, the grace of God was upon Him."

Luke 2:39,40

Hail Mary

Glory Be

Glory be to the Father, and to the Son, and to the Holy Spirit.
As it was in the beginning, is now, and ever shall be, world without end. Amen.

Fifth Joyful Mystery

The Finding Of Jesus In The Temple

Our Father

Every year His parents went to Jerusalem
for the feast of the Passover.

Luke 2:41

Hail Mary

While His parents were returning home, the boy Jesus stayed behind in Jerusalem, but they were unaware of it.

Luke 2:43

Hail Mary

When they did not find Him, they went back to Jerusalem. After three days they found Him.

Luke 2:45,46

Hail Mary

They found Him in the temple courts, sitting among the teachers, listening to them and asking them questions.

Luke 2:46

Hail Mary

Everyone who heard Him was amazed
at His understanding and His answers.

Luke 2:47

Hail Mary

His mother said, "Son, why have you treated us like this? Your father and I have been searching for You."

Luke 2:48

Hail Mary

"Why were you searching for Me?
Didn't you know I had to be in My Father's house?"

Luke 2:49

Hail Mary

They did not understand
what He was saying.

Luke 2:50

Hail Mary

Then He went down to Nazareth with them
and was obedient to them.

Luke 2:51

Hail Mary

Jesus grew in wisdom and stature,
and in favor with God and men.

Luke 2:52

Hail Mary

Glory Be

Glory be to the Father, and to the Son, and to the Holy Spirit.
As it was in the beginning, is now, and ever shall be, world without end. Amen.

Hail Holy Queen

Hail, Holy Queen,
Mother of Mercy, our life, our sweetness, and our hope!
To you we cry, poor banished children of Eve;
to you we send up our sighs,
mourning and weeping in this valley of tears.
Turn then, most gracious advocate,
your eyes of mercy toward us;
and after this our exile,
show us the blessed fruit of your womb, Jesus.
O clement, O loving, O sweet Virgin Mary.

V. Pray for us, O holy Mother of God.

R. That we may be made worthy of the promises of Christ.

The Mysteries of Light

First Mystery of Light

Jesus' Baptism in the Jordan

Our Father

And this was his message:
"After me will come one more powerful than I."

Mark 1:7

Hail Mary

"The thongs of whose sandals
I am not worthy to stoop down and untie."

Mark 1:7

Hail Mary

"I baptize you with water,
but He will baptize you with the Holy Spirit."

Mark 1:8

Hail Mary

The next day John saw Jesus coming toward him and said, "Look, the Lamb of God, who takes away the sins of the world!"

John 1:29

Hail Mary

At that time Jesus came from Nazareth in Galilee and was baptized by John in the Jordan.

Mark 1:9

Hail Mary

"I myself did not know Him, but the reason I came baptizing with water was that He might be revealed to Israel."

John 1:31

Hail Mary

As Jesus was coming up out of the water, John saw heaven being torn open and the Spirit descending on Him like a dove.

Mark 1:10

Hail Mary

"The man on whom you see the Spirit come down and remain is He who will baptize with the Holy Spirit."

John 1:33

Hail Mary

And a voice came from heaven: "You are My Son, whom I love; with You I am well pleased."

Mark 1:11

Hail Mary

At once the Spirit sent Him out into the desert.

Mark 1:12

Hail Mary

Glory Be

Glory be to the Father, and to the Son, and to the Holy Spirit.
As it was in the beginning, is now, and ever shall be, world without end. Amen.

Second Mystery of Light

The Manifestation of Jesus

Our Father

On the third day
a wedding took place at Cana in Galilee.

John 2:1

Hail Mary

Jesus' mother was there, and Jesus and His disciples
had also been invited to the wedding.

John 2:1,2

Hail Mary

When the wine was gone, Jesus' mother said to Him,
"They have no more wine."

John 2:3

Hail Mary

"Dear woman, why do you involve Me?" Jesus replied.
"My time has not yet come."

John 2:4

Hail Mary

His mother said to the servants,
"Do whatever He tells you."

John 2:5

Hail Mary

Jesus said to the servants, "Fill the jars with water"; so they filled them to the brim.

John 2:7

Hail Mary

Then He told them, "Now draw some out and take it to the master of the banquet."

John 2:8

Hail Mary

The master of the banquet tasted the water that had been turned into wine.

John 2:9

Hail Mary

Then he said, "Everyone brings out the choice wine first and then the cheaper wine; but you have saved the best for last."

John 2:10

Hail Mary

This, the first of His miraculous signs, Jesus performed at Cana in Galilee. He thus revealed His glory.

John 2:11

Hail Mary

Glory Be

Glory be to the Father, and to the Son, and to the Holy Spirit.
As it was in the beginning, is now, and ever shall be, world without end. Amen.

Third Mystery of Light

The Call to Conversion

Our Father

"The time has come," Jesus said. "The kingdom of God is near. Repent and believe the good news."

Mark 1:15

Hail Mary

As Jesus walked beside the Sea of Galilee, He saw Simon and his brother Andrew casting a net into the lake.

Mark 1:16

Hail Mary

"Come, follow Me," Jesus said,
"And I will make you fishers of men."

Mark 1:17

Hail Mary

At once they left their nets and followed Him.

Mark 1:18

Hail Mary

Some men came bringing a paralytic. They could not get him to Jesus because of the crowd, they made an opening in the roof above Jesus and lowered the mat the man was lying on.

Mark 2:4

Hail Mary

When Jesus saw their faith, He said to the paralytic, "Son, your sins are forgiven."

Mark 2:5

Hail Mary

Once again Jesus went out beside the lake. As He went along, He saw Levi sitting at the tax collector's booth.

Mark 2: 13,14

Hail Mary

"Follow Me," Jesus told him, and Levi got up and followed Him.

Mark 2:14

Hail Mary

When the teachers of the law who were Pharisees saw Him eating with the "sinners" they asked His disciples: "Why does he eat with tax collectors and 'sinners'?"

Mark 2:16

Hail Mary

Jesus said to them, "It is not the healthy who need a doctor, but the sick. I have not come to call the righteous, but sinners."

Mark 2:17

Hail Mary

Glory Be

Glory be to the Father, and to the Son, and to the Holy Spirit.
As it was in the beginning, is now, and ever shall be, world without end. Amen.

Fourth Mystery of Light

The Transfiguration of Jesus

Our Father

Jesus took Peter, James and John with Him and led them up a high mountain, where they were all alone.

Mark 9:2

Hail Mary

As He was praying, the appearance of His face changed, and His clothes became as bright as a flash of lightning.

Luke 9:29

Hail Mary

Two men, Moses and Elijah, appeared in glorious splendor, talking with Jesus.

Luke 9:30, 31

Hail Mary

They spoke about His departure, which He was about to bring to fulfillment at Jerusalem.

Luke 9:31

Hail Mary

Peter said to Jesus, "Rabbi, it is good for us to be here. Let us put up three shelters—one for You, Moses and Elijah."

Mark 9:5

Hail Mary

Then a cloud appeared and enveloped them, and a voice came from the cloud: "This is My Son, whom I love. Listen to Him!"

Mark 9:7

Hail Mary

When the disciples heard this,
they fell facedown to the ground, terrified.

Matthew 17:6

Hail Mary

But Jesus came and touched them.
"Get up," He said. "Don't be afraid.

Matthew 17:7

Hail Mary

When they looked up, they saw no one except Jesus.

Matthew 17:8

Hail Mary

As they were coming down the mountain, Jesus instructed them, "Don't tell anyone what you have seen, until the Son of Man has been raised from the dead."

Matthew 17:9

Hail Mary

Glory Be

Glory be to the Father, and to the Son, and to the Holy Spirit.
As it was in the beginning, is now, and ever shall be, world without end. Amen.

Fifth Mystery of Light

The Paschal Mystery

Our Father

It was just before the Passover feast: Jesus knew that the time had come for Him to leave this world and go to the Father.

John 13:1

Hail Mary

Having loved His own who were in the world, He now showed them the full extent of His love.

John 13:1

Hail Mary

"Go into the city to a certain man and tell him, 'The teacher says: My appointed time is near. I am going to celebrate the Passover with my disciples at your house.'"

Matthew 26:18

Hail Mary

When evening came, Jesus arrived with the twelve.

Mark 14:17

Hail Mary

And Jesus said to them. "I have eagerly desired to eat this Passover with you before I suffer."

Luke 22:15

Hail Mary

While they were eating, Jesus took bread, gave thanks
and broke it, and gave it to His disciples, saying,
"Take it; this is My body."

Mark 14:22

Hail Mary

Then He took the cup, gave thanks and offered it to
them, saying, "Drink from it, all of you."

Matthew 26:27

Hail Mary

"This is My blood of the covenant, which is poured out
for many for the forgiveness of sins."

Matthew 26:28

Hail Mary

"I will not drink of this fruit of the vine from now on
until that day when I drink it anew with you in My
Father's Kingdom.

Matthew 26:29

Hail Mary

When they had sung a hymn,
they went out to the Mount of Olives.

Mark 14:26

Hail Mary

Glory Be

Glory be to the Father, and to the Son, and to the
Holy Spirit.
As it was in the beginning, is now, and ever shall be,
world without end. Amen.

Hail Holy Queen

Hail, Holy Queen,
Mother of Mercy, our life, our sweetness, and our hope!
To you we cry, poor banished children of Eve;
to you we send up our sighs,
mourning and weeping in this valley of tears.
Turn then, most gracious advocate,
your eyes of mercy toward us;
and after this our exile,
show us the blessed fruit of your womb, Jesus.
O clement, O loving, O sweet Virgin Mary.

V. Pray for us, O holy Mother of God.

R. That we may be made worthy of the promises of Christ

The Sorrowful Mysteries

First Sorrowful Mystery

The Agony In The Garden

Our Father

Then Jesus went with His disciples to a place called Gethsemane. He began to be sorrowful and troubled.

Matthew 26:36,37

Hail Mary

"My soul is overwhelmed with sorrow to the point of death. Stay here and keep watch with Me."

Matthew 26:38

Hail Mary

Going a little farther,
He fell with His face to the ground and prayed.

Matthew 26:39

Hail Mary

"My Father, if it is possible, may this cup be taken from Me. Yet not as I will, but as You will.

Matthew 26:39

Hail Mary

An angel from heaven appeared to Him
and strengthened Him.

Luke 22:43

Hail Mary

Being in anguish,
He prayed more earnestly.

Luke 22:44

Hail Mary

His sweat was like drops of blood
falling to the ground.

Luke 22:44

Hail Mary

Then He returned to His disciples and found them sleeping.
"Could you men not keep watch with Me for one hour?"

Matthew 26:40

Hail Mary

"Watch and pray
so that you will not fall into temptation."

Matthew 26:41

Hail Mary

"The spirit is willing,
but the body is weak."

Matthew 26:41

Hail Mary

Glory Be

Glory be to the Father, and to the Son, and to the
Holy Spirit.
As it was in the beginning, is now, and ever shall be,
world without end. Amen.

Second Sorrowful Mystery

The Scourging At The Pillar

Our Father

They bound Jesus,
led Him away and handed Him over to Pilate.

Mark 15:1

Hail Mary

"If you are the Christ,"
they said, "Tell us."

Luke 22:67

Hail Mary

Jesus answered, "If I tell you, you will not believe Me.
From now on the Son of Man will be seated at the
right hand of the Mighty God."

Luke 22:67,69

Hail Mary

They all asked,
"Are you then the Son of God."

Luke 22:70

Hail Mary

He replied, "You are right in saying I am."

Luke 22:70

Hail Mary

"Are You
the King of the Jews?" asked Pilate.

Mark 15:2

Hail Mary

Jesus said, "My Kingdom is not of this world.
You are right in saying I am a King."

John 18:36,37

Hail Mary

"For this I came into the world, to testify to the truth.
Everyone on the side of the truth listens to Me."

John 18:37

Hail Mary

"What is truth?" Pilate asked. With this he went out
to the Jews and said, "I find no basis for a charge
against Him."

John 18:38

Hail Mary

Then Pilate took Jesus
and had Him flogged.

John 19:1

Hail Mary

Glory Be

Glory be to the Father, and to the Son, and to the
Holy Spirit.
As it was in the beginning, is now, and ever shall be,
world without end. Amen.

Third Sorrowful Mystery

The Crowning With Thorns

Our Father

The soldiers led Jesus away into the Praetorium.
They put a purple robe on Him.

Mark 15:16,17

Hail Mary

The soldiers twisted together a crown of thorns
and put it on His head.

John 19:2

Hail Mary

They put a staff in His right hand and knelt in front
of Him and mocked Him. "Hail, King of the Jews!"
they said.

Matthew 27:29

Hail Mary

They spit on Him, and took the staff and struck Him
on the head again and again.

Matthew 27:30

Hail Mary

When Pilate saw that he was getting nowhere, he took
water and washed his hands. "I am innocent of this
man's blood."

Matthew 27:24

Hail Mary

When Jesus came out wearing the crown of thorns and the purple robe, Pilate said to them, "Here is the man!"

John 19:5

Hail Mary

But they shouted, "Take Him away! Take Him away! Crucify Him!"

John 19:15

Hail Mary

"Why? What crime has He committed?" asked Pilate.

Mark 15:14

Hail Mary

"Shall I crucify your King?" Pilate asked.

John 19:15

Hail Mary

"We have no king but Caesar," the chief priests answered.
Finally Pilate handed Him over to them to be crucified.

John 19:15,16

Hail Mary

Glory Be

Glory be to the Father, and to the Son, and to the Holy Spirit.
As it was in the beginning, is now, and ever shall be, world without end. Amen.

Fourth Sorrowful Mystery

The Carrying Of The Cross

Our Father

Then He said to them all: "If anyone would come after Me, he must deny himself."

Luke 9:23

Hail Mary

"And take up his cross daily and follow Me."

Luke 9:23

Hail Mary

Carrying His own cross, He went out to the place of the Skull.

John 19:17

Hail Mary

As they led Him away, they seized Simon from Cyrene, and put the cross on him, and made him carry it behind Jesus.

Luke 23:26

Hail Mary

"Take My yoke upon you and learn from Me."

Matthew 11:29

Hail Mary

"For I am gentle
and humble in heart."

Matthew 11:29

Hail Mary

"You will find rest for your souls. For My yoke is easy
and My burden is light."

Matthew 11:29,30

Hail Mary

A large number of people followed Him, including women
who mourned and wailed for Him.

Luke 23:27

Hail Mary

Jesus turned and said to them, "Daughters of Jerusalem,
do not weep for Me; weep for yourselves and
for your children."

Luke 23:28

Hail Mary

"For if men do these things when the tree is green,
what will happen when it is dry?"

Luke 23:31

Hail Mary

Glory Be

Glory be to the Father, and to the Son, and to the
Holy Spirit.
As it was in the beginning, is now, and ever shall be,
world without end. Amen.

Fifth Sorrowful Mystery

The Crucifixion

Our Father

When they came to the place called Skull,
there they crucified Him.

Luke 23:33

Hail Mary

Jesus said, "Father, forgive them,
for they do not know what they are doing."

Luke 23:34

Hail Mary

The other criminal said,
"Jesus remember me when you come into
your Kingdom."

Luke 23:40,42

Hail Mary

Jesus answered him, "I tell you the truth,
today you will be with Me in paradise."

Luke 23:43

Hail Mary

Near the cross of Jesus stood His mother,
and the disciple whom He loved.

John 19:25,26

Hail Mary

He said to His mother, "Dear woman, here is your son,"
and to the disciple, "Here is your mother."

John 19:26,27

Hail Mary

From that time on,
this disciple took her into his home.

John 19:27

Hail Mary

For the sun stopped shining
and the curtain of the Temple was torn in two.

Luke 23:44

Hail Mary

Jesus called out with a loud voice,
"Father, into Your hands I commit My Spirit."

Luke 23:46

Hail Mary

When He had said this,
He breathed His last.

Luke 23:46

Hail Mary

Glory Be

Glory be to the Father, and to the Son, and to the Holy Spirit.
As it was in the beginning, is now, and ever shall be,
world without end. Amen.

Hail Holy Queen

Hail, Holy Queen,
Mother of Mercy, our life, our sweetness, and our hope!
To you we cry, poor banished children of Eve;
to you we send up our sighs,
mourning and weeping in this valley of tears.
Turn then, most gracious advocate,
your eyes of mercy toward us;
and after this our exile,
show us the blessed fruit of your womb, Jesus.
O clement, O loving, O sweet Virgin Mary.

V. Pray for us, O holy Mother of God.

R. That we may be made worthy of the promises of Christ.

The Glorious Mysteries

First Glorious Mystery

The Resurrection

Our Father

"You will grieve,
but your grief will turn to joy."

John 16:20

Hail Mary

"But I will see you again and you will rejoice,
and no one will take away your joy."

John 16:22

Hail Mary

Very early in the morning, the women took the spices
they had prepared and went to the tomb.

Luke 24:1

Hail Mary

An angel of the Lord came down from heaven and
rolled back the stone and sat on it.

Matthew 28:2

Hail Mary

"I know that you are looking for Jesus.
He is not here."

Matthew 28:5,6

Hail Mary

"He has risen.
Come and see the place where He lay."

Matthew 28:6

Hail Mary

"He is going ahead of you into Galilee.
There you will see Him."

Matthew 28:7

Hail Mary

So the women hurried away from the tomb,
afraid yet filled with joy.

Matthew 28:8

Hail Mary

"I am the resurrection and the life.
He who believes in Me will live, even though he dies."

John 11:25

Hail Mary

"And whoever lives
and believes in Me will never die."

John 11:26

Hail Mary

Glory Be

Glory be to the Father, and to the Son, and to the
Holy Spirit.
As it was in the beginning, is now, and ever shall be,
world without end. Amen.

Second Glorious Mystery

The Ascension

Our Father

When He had led them out to the vicinity of Bethany,
He lifted up His hands and blessed them.

Luke 24:50

Hail Mary

Then Jesus came to them and said, "All authority in
heaven and on earth has been given to Me."

Matthew 28:18

Hail Mary

"Therefore go and make disciples
of all nations."

Matthew 28:19

Hail Mary

"Baptizing them in the name of the Father,
and of the Son and of the Holy Spirit."

Matthew 28:19

Hail Mary

"Teaching them to obey everything
I have commanded you."

Matthew 28:20

Hail Mary

"Whoever believes
and is baptized will be saved."

Mark 16:16

Hail Mary

"Whoever does not believe
will be condemned."

Mark 16:16

Hail Mary

"And surely I am with you always,
to the very end of the age."

Matthew 28:20

Hail Mary

After He said this,
He was taken up before their very eyes.

Acts 1:9

Hail Mary

He was taken up into heaven
and He sat at the right hand of God.

Mark 16:19

Hail Mary

Glory Be

Glory be to the Father, and to the Son, and to the Holy Spirit.
As it was in the beginning, is now, and ever shall be, world without end. Amen.

Third Glorious Mystery

The Descent Of The Holy Spirit

Our Father

When the day of Pentecost came,
they were all together in one place.

Acts 2:1

Hail Mary

Suddenly a sound like the blowing of a violent wind came
from heaven and filled the whole house.

Acts 2:2

Hail Mary

They saw what seemed to be tongues of fire
that separated and came to rest on each of them.

Acts 2:3

Hail Mary

All of them
were filled with the Holy Spirit.

Acts 2:4

Hail Mary

Now there were staying in Jerusalem God–fearing Jews
from every nation under heaven.

Acts 2:5

Hail Mary

Peter stood up with the Eleven,
raised his voice and addressed the crowd.

Acts 2:14

Hail Mary

"Repent and be baptized,
and you will receive the gifts of the Holy Spirit."

Acts 2:38

Hail Mary

Those who accepted his message were baptized,
and about three thousand were added to their number
that day.

Acts 2:41

Hail Mary

They devoted themselves to the Apostles' teaching, to the
breaking of bread, and to prayer.

Acts 2:42

Hail Mary

And the Lord added to their number daily
those who were being saved.

Acts 2:47

Hail Mary

Glory Be

Glory be to the Father, and to the Son, and to the
Holy Spirit.
As it was in the beginning, is now, and ever shall be,
world without end. Amen.

Fourth Glorious Mystery

The Assumption

Our Father

Then God's temple in heaven
was opened.

Revelation 11:19

Hail Mary

"Like a lily among thorns
is my darling among the maidens."

Song of Songs 2:2

Hail Mary

"All beautiful you are, my darling;
there is no flaw in you."

Song of Songs 4:7

Hail Mary

All glorious is the princess within her chamber;
her gown is interwoven with gold.

Psalm 45:13

Hail Mary

"Arise, my darling, my beautiful one,
and come with Me."

Song of Songs 2:10

Hail Mary

"See the winter is past;
the rains are over and gone."

Song of Songs 2:11

Hail Mary

"Flowers appear on the earth; the season of singing
has come,
the cooing of doves is heard in our land."

Song of Songs 2:12

Hail Mary

"The fig tree forms its early fruit;
the blossoming vines spread their fragrance."

Song of Songs 2:13

Hail Mary

In embroidered garments
she is led to the King.

Psalm 45:14

Hail Mary

"He has taken me to the banquet hall,
and His banner over me is love."

Song of Songs 2:4

Hail Mary

Glory Be

Glory be to the Father, and to the Son, and to the
Holy Spirit.
As it was in the beginning, is now, and ever shall be,
world without end. Amen.

Fifth Glorious Mystery

The Coronation

Our Father

A great and wondrous sign
appeared in heaven.

Revelation 12:1

Hail Mary

A woman clothed with the sun, with the moon under her feet and a crown of twelve stars on her head.

Revelation 12:1

Hail Mary

"Who is this that appears like the dawn, fair as the moon, bright as the sun,
majestic as the stars in procession?"

Song of Songs 6:10

Hail Mary

"I am a rose of Sharon, a lily of the valleys."

Song of Songs 2:1

Hail Mary

"My heart is stirred by a noble theme
as I recite my verses for the King."

Psalm 45:1

Hail Mary

"Your lips have been anointed with grace,
since God has blessed you forever."

Psalm 45:2

Hail Mary

"Listen to me; blessed are those who keep my ways.
Listen to my instruction and be wise; do not ignore it."

Proverbs 8:32,33

Hail Mary

"For whoever finds me finds life
and receives favor from the Lord."

Proverbs 8:35

Hail Mary

"I will sing
the Lord's great love forever."

Psalm 89:1

Hail Mary

"With my mouth I will make your faithfulness
known through all generations."

Psalm 89:1

Hail Mary

Glory Be

Glory be to the Father, and to the Son, and to the
Holy Spirit.
As it was in the beginning, is now, and ever shall be
world without end. Amen.

Hail Holy Queen

Hail, Holy Queen,
Mother of Mercy, our life, our sweetness, and our hope!
To you we cry, poor banished children of Eve;
to you we send up our sighs,
mourning and weeping in this valley of tears.
Turn then, most gracious advocate,
your eyes of mercy toward us;
and after this our exile,
show us the blessed fruit of your womb, Jesus.
O clement, O loving, O sweet Virgin Mary.

V. Pray for us, O holy Mother of God.

R. That we may be made worthy of the promises of Christ.